CARGO SHIPS

BOATS & SHIPS

Jason Cooper

The Rourke Corporation, Inc.
Vero Beach, Florida 32964

PHOTO CREDITS:
Courtesy Chevron Corporation: pages 10, 13; © Calvin Larsen/Affordable Photo Stock: page 4, page 18; © Craig Lovell: page 12; © James Rowan: pages 8, 15, 21; courtesy Shell Oil Corporation: page 7; courtesy Star Clippers: page 17; © Lynn M. Stone: cover, title page

CREATIVE SERVICES:
East Coast Studios, Merritt Island, Florida

EDITORIAL SERVICES:
Susan Albury

Library of Congress Cataloging-in-Publication Data

Cooper, Jason, 1942-
Cargo ships / by Jason Cooper.
p. cm. — (Boats)
Includes index.
Summary: Presents the history, parts, uses, and types of cargo ships, which transport goods around the world by sea.
ISBN 0-86593-561-0
1. Cargo ships—Juvenile literature. 2. Freight and freightage—Juvenile literature.
[1. Cargo ships.]
I. Title II. Series: Cooper, Jason, 1942- Boats & ships
HE566.F7C66 1999
623.8' 245—dc21 99-15112
CIP

Printed in the USA

TABLE OF CONTENTS

CARGO SHIPS

Cargo ships are designed to carry the many different goods we call **cargo** (KAR go), or freight.

Cargo ships are often called **freighters** (FRAYT urz). They carry such freight as wheat and wood chips, corn and coffee, plastics and petroleum, meat and machines.

Pilot boats help guide big ships into and out of ports. Here a pilot boat moves toward the tanker Keystone Canyon.

Cargo ships are seagoing **vessels** (VEH sulz). The largest of them are among the largest ships afloat. The biggest ocean liner, for example, is about 1,000 feet (305 meters) long. The largest cargo ships are **supertankers** (SOO pur tang kurz). They carry oil. The largest supertankers are more than 1,500 feet (457 meters) long! That is the length of more than four football fields end to end.

Cargo ships are sometimes called merchant ships. Merchants are those who sell or trade goods. The word *merchant* helps explain the job of cargo ships. A nation's **fleet** (FLEET), or total number, of cargo ships is called its merchant marine fleet.

An oil tanker awaits loading at docks by an oil refinery. Refineries change crude oil—oil from the ground—into gasoline, engine oil, and other products.

TOYOTA

THE WORK OF CARGO SHIPS

Countries that make many products need places in which to sell them. Those places are often other countries. Cargo ships are an important way to move goods from one country to another.

Countries that do make many products, like the United States and Japan, use large fleets of cargo ships. Those ships transport many of the goods these and other nations produce. For example, many autos in Japan are transported to other countries aboard cargo ships.

A Japanese auto carrier ship lies at anchor in Boston Harbor, Massachusetts.

PARTS OF A CARGO SHIP

The main part of any ship is its **hull** (HUHL), or shell. Some of the newest and largest oil tankers have two hulls. One hull is inside the other. If the outer hull cracks, the inner hull may still protect the ship's cargo.

The hull has several decks, or floors, built into it. The main deck fits across the top of the hull, like a cover on a swimming pool. Cargo is stored in **holds** (HOLDZ) built into the hull.

From high on the bridge, the captain can look across the bow of this tanker ship and guide the ship out to sea.

This freighter carries box cars on Lake Titicaca in Bolivia.

The deck of this tanker is a jumble of pipes.

Above the main deck are additional structures, including the **bridge** (BRIJ). The bridge is the captain's control room.

Cargo ships are powered by engines in rooms well below the main deck. The largest, fastest cargo ships have steam **turbine** (TUR bun) engines. Others are powered by diesel or gas turbine engines.

The ship propeller, or propellers, are linked to the power produced by the engine. The propeller blades spin in the water like a giant fan. The propeller's motion pushes the ship along.

The smokestack and houselike building above the main deck make up this cargo ship's superstructure. Part of the ship's rudder can be seen above the white foam.

IOANNIS-P

THE FIRST CARGO SHIPS

The first cargo ships appeared at least 4,500 years ago in Egypt. They were wooden sailing ships. The largest were about 150 feet (46 meters) long.

Nearly all cargo ships were sailing ships until the steam engine was invented in the mid-1800s.

Many of the sailing ships carried a few passengers as well as cargo. Packet ships were well-known passenger-cargo ships in America.

The fast, cargo-carrying clipper ships of the 1800s looked much like this modern clipper-style ship.

EVERGREEN
EVER LAUREL

Some of the most beautiful ships ever were the great cargo-carrying clipper ships of the 1800s. Some raised as many as 35 sails! However, by the early 1900s, the clippers and other masted ships were finished. Steamboats had taken over the cargo business.

In the 20th century, cargo ships became bigger and stronger. They also began to **specialize** (SPEH shul ize). Ships began to be designed for only certain kinds of cargo. No longer was freight of all kinds always loaded on one ship.

Modern freighters are built to sail safely in seas all over the world. There is always the risk, however, of a tanker running onto ground and spilling oil into the sea.

KINDS OF CARGO SHIPS

Some freighters still carry a variety of cargo. Most cargo ships are designed to haul one type.

One of the first special cargo ships was the tanker. A tanker has a hull like a giant ice cube tray. Each "cube" holds oil or some other liquid.

The largest of the supertankers can hold more than one billion pounds (453 million kilograms) of oil!

A dry-bulk carrier, loaded with ore, works its way through canal locks in Sault Saint Marie, Michigan.

J. L. MAUTHE
THE
INTERLAKE
STEAMSHIP CO.

Dry-bulk cargo ships are built to carry sand, sugar, grain, iron ore, powder, salt, wood chips, and other loose dry goods.

Container ships carry cargo that has been put into huge steel boxes called containers. Containers can be unloaded from a ship onto train cars.

At least part of the cargo on a roll-on/roll-off ship is made up of containers with wheels or autos, trucks, or buses.

Lighter Aboard Ships (LASH) carry barges called **lighters** (LIE turz). The lighters are stacked with cargo. LASH ships unload their lighter barges for tugboats to haul away.

GLOSSARY

bridge (BRIJ) — a raised platform from which a ship can be operated and watched

cargo (KAR go) — those goods that a ship brings abroad; freight

fleet (FLEET) — a group of ships

freighter (FRAYT ur) — a ship that hauls cargo of one kind or another

hold (HOLD) — a storage area within the hull of a ship

hull (HUHL) — the floating shell of a boat or ship

lighter (LIE tur) — a flat-bottomed barge

specialize (SPEH shul ize) — to make ready for one use rather than several

supertanker (SOO pur tang kur) — a ship designed to carry oil or other liquids

turbine (TUR bun) — a type of engine usually using a series of curved blades in its operation

vessel (VEH sul) — a boat or ship

INDEX

FURTHER READING

Find out more about cargo ships with these helpful books:

- Butterfield, Moira. *Look Inside Cross Sections Ships.* Dorling Kindersley, 1994
- Graham, Ian. *Boats, Ships, Submarines and Other Floating Machines.* Kingfisher, 1993
- Humble, Richard. *Submarines and Ships.* Viking, 1997